EMMANUEL JOSEPH

Echoes of the Future, A Philosophical Journey Through History and Innovation

Copyright © 2025 by Emmanuel Joseph

All rights reserved. No part of this publication may be reproduced, stored or transmitted in any form or by any means, electronic, mechanical, photocopying, recording, scanning, or otherwise without written permission from the publisher. It is illegal to copy this book, post it to a website, or distribute it by any other means without permission.

First edition

This book was professionally typeset on Reedsy.
Find out more at reedsy.com

Contents

1	Chapter 1: The Dawn of Civilization	1
2	Chapter 2: The Age of Enlightenment	3
3	Chapter 3: The Industrial Revolution	5
4	Chapter 4: The Digital Age	7
5	Chapter 5: The Quest for Sustainability	9
6	Chapter 6: The Rise of Artificial Intelligence	11
7	Chapter 7: The Exploration of Space	13
8	Chapter 8: The Evolution of Communication	15
9	Chapter 9: The Future of Education	17
10	Chapter 10: The Ethical Dimensions of Innovation	19
11	Chapter 11: The Role of Creativity and Art	21
12	Chapter 12: The Philosophical Pursuit of Knowledge	23
13	Chapter 13: The Interplay of Science and Society	25
14	Chapter 14: The Impact of Globalization	27
15	Chapter 15: The Future of Humanity	29

1

Chapter 1: The Dawn of Civilization

The birth of civilization marked a significant turning point in human history. Ancient cultures flourished along riverbanks, where the fertile soil allowed communities to grow and prosper. People gathered to share their knowledge, laying the foundations for the complex societies we know today. The invention of writing enabled the preservation of ideas, while monumental architecture symbolized the power and ambition of early rulers. This period was a time of exploration and discovery, as humanity began to understand the world around them and their place within it.

As communities expanded, so did the need for organized governance and social structures. The first city-states emerged, with rulers who sought to maintain order and protect their people. The development of laws and the establishment of trade routes facilitated the exchange of goods and ideas, fostering cultural and technological advancements. The rise of agriculture allowed for surplus food production, which in turn supported population growth and urbanization. This era laid the groundwork for the complex societies that would follow.

The dawn of civilization also saw the emergence of religion and spirituality as central aspects of human life. Ancient peoples created myths and legends to explain natural phenomena and the mysteries of existence. Temples and religious rituals became integral parts of daily life, reflecting the belief in a higher power that governed the universe. These early spiritual practices provided a sense of order and purpose, guiding individuals and communities in their quest for meaning and understanding.

Art and creativity flourished during this time, as people sought to express their experiences and emotions through various mediums. The creation of pottery, sculpture, and painting showcased the ingenuity and skill of early artisans. Storytelling and oral traditions preserved the wisdom of the ages, passing down knowledge and culture from one generation to the next. The dawn of civilization was a period of immense growth and innovation, setting the stage for the future achievements of humanity.

2

Chapter 2: The Age of Enlightenment

The Age of Enlightenment was a period of intellectual and philosophical growth that transformed societies across Europe and beyond. This era saw the emergence of new ideas that challenged traditional beliefs and institutions, paving the way for modern thought and progress. Enlightenment thinkers advocated for reason, science, and individual rights, seeking to improve the human condition through knowledge and understanding. Their ideas laid the foundation for the political, social, and technological advancements that would shape the modern world.

Philosophers such as John Locke, Voltaire, and Immanuel Kant played pivotal roles in shaping Enlightenment thought. They questioned the authority of the church and monarchy, advocating for the separation of powers and the establishment of democratic governance. The concept of natural rights, which held that all individuals were entitled to life, liberty, and property, gained traction during this time. These ideas inspired revolutionary movements and the creation of constitutions that sought to protect individual freedoms and promote justice.

The scientific revolution, which began during the Renaissance, gained momentum in the Age of Enlightenment. Pioneers like Isaac Newton, Galileo Galilei, and René Descartes made groundbreaking discoveries that expanded humanity's understanding of the natural world. The scientific method, based on observation and experimentation, became the standard for acquiring knowledge. This shift towards empiricism and rationality led to significant advancements in fields such as astronomy, physics, and medicine, transforming the way people perceived the universe and their place within it.

The Age of Enlightenment also saw the flourishing of art, literature, and culture. Writers like Mary Wollstonecraft, Jean-Jacques Rousseau, and Denis Diderot explored themes of human nature, society, and morality in their works. The period was marked by a spirit of curiosity and exploration, as people sought to uncover the mysteries of the world and expand their intellectual horizons. The Enlightenment's emphasis on reason, progress, and individual rights laid the groundwork for the modern era, shaping the values and institutions that continue to influence contemporary society.

3

Chapter 3: The Industrial Revolution

The Industrial Revolution was a period of rapid technological advancement and economic transformation that began in the late 18th century. This era saw the emergence of new manufacturing processes, powered by innovations such as the steam engine and mechanized textile production. The shift from agrarian economies to industrialized ones brought profound changes to societies, altering the way people lived and worked. Urbanization accelerated as people flocked to cities in search of employment, and new social classes emerged, reflecting the changing economic landscape.

The development of factories and mass production techniques revolutionized industries, making goods more accessible and affordable. Innovations in transportation, such as the steam locomotive and the construction of extensive railway networks, facilitated the movement of people and goods across vast distances. These advancements spurred economic growth and global trade, creating new markets and opportunities for entrepreneurs and investors. The Industrial Revolution transformed societies, ushering in an era of unprecedented economic prosperity and technological progress.

However, the rapid pace of industrialization also brought significant challenges. The rise of factory labor led to harsh working conditions, with long hours, low wages, and little regard for worker safety. The exploitation of child labor and the lack of labor regulations highlighted the need for social and political reforms. The environmental impact of industrialization, including pollution and deforestation, became increasingly apparent. These issues prompted the emergence of labor movements and calls for government intervention to address the social and economic inequalities resulting from industrialization.

The Industrial Revolution also had a profound impact on culture and society. The rise of the middle class and increased access to education and leisure activities contributed to the flourishing of arts and literature. Writers like Charles Dickens and Elizabeth Gaskell documented the experiences of the working class, shedding light on the social injustices of the time. The period was marked by a sense of optimism and belief in progress, as technological advancements promised to improve living standards and reshape the world. The Industrial Revolution set the stage for the modern era, shaping the economic, social, and cultural landscape of contemporary society.

4

Chapter 4: The Digital Age

The advent of the digital age in the late 20th and early 21st centuries marked a new chapter in human history, characterized by rapid advancements in technology and communication. The development of computers, the internet, and mobile devices transformed the way people lived, worked, and interacted with one another. This era of unprecedented connectivity and information exchange revolutionized industries, reshaped economies, and redefined the boundaries of human knowledge and creativity.

The rise of the internet enabled global communication and access to information on an unprecedented scale. Social media platforms, search engines, and e-commerce websites became integral parts of daily life, connecting people across the world and facilitating the exchange of ideas and goods. The digital age also saw the emergence of new forms of entertainment and media, with streaming services, video games, and online content creators capturing the imagination of audiences worldwide. The proliferation of digital technology democratized information and empowered individuals to share their voices and stories.

The digital age brought about significant changes in the workforce and economy. Automation, artificial intelligence, and machine learning transformed industries, increasing efficiency and productivity while also raising concerns about job displacement and the future of work. The gig economy emerged, offering new opportunities for freelance and remote work but also highlighting the need for social protections and labor rights. The digital revolution spurred innovation and entrepreneurship, with tech startups and digital platforms driving economic growth and reshaping traditional business models.

The digital age also posed new challenges and ethical dilemmas. Issues such as data privacy, cybersecurity, and digital addiction became increasingly prominent as people grappled with the implications of living in an interconnected world. The spread of misinformation and the rise of echo chambers on social media platforms raised concerns about the impact of technology on democracy and public discourse. As society navigated the complexities of the digital age, there was a growing recognition of the need to balance technological progress with ethical considerations and human values.

5

Chapter 5: The Quest for Sustainability

In the 21st century, the quest for sustainability emerged as a critical global challenge. As the impact of human activity on the environment became increasingly evident, there was a growing awareness of the need to balance economic growth with ecological preservation. Climate change, deforestation, and pollution highlighted the urgent need for sustainable practices and policies to protect the planet for future generations. This chapter explores the evolution of the sustainability movement and the innovative solutions that have been developed to address environmental challenges.

The concept of sustainability is rooted in the idea of meeting the needs of the present without compromising the ability of future generations to meet their own needs. This requires a holistic approach that considers the interconnectedness of economic, social, and environmental systems. Governments, businesses, and individuals have increasingly embraced sustainability as a guiding principle, recognizing the importance of responsible resource management, renewable energy, and environmental conservation. The transition to a more sustainable future involves rethinking traditional practices and adopting innovative technologies and strategies.

Renewable energy sources, such as solar, wind, and hydroelectric power, have gained prominence as alternatives to fossil fuels. These clean energy solutions offer the potential to reduce greenhouse gas emissions and mitigate the effects of climate change. Advances in energy storage and smart grid technology have improved the efficiency and reliability of renewable energy systems. Additionally, sustainable transportation options, such as electric vehicles and public transit, have emerged as key components of efforts to reduce carbon footprints and promote green mobility.

The quest for sustainability also involves addressing issues of social equity and justice. Environmental degradation often disproportionately affects vulnerable communities, exacerbating existing inequalities. The concept of environmental justice emphasizes the need to ensure that all people, regardless of their background, have access to clean air, water, and a healthy environment. Sustainable development initiatives seek to create inclusive and resilient communities, promoting economic opportunities and improving quality of life while safeguarding natural resources.

6

Chapter 6: The Rise of Artificial Intelligence

The rise of artificial intelligence (AI) represents one of the most transformative developments of the 21st century. AI technologies, which enable machines to perform tasks that typically require human intelligence, have the potential to revolutionize industries, enhance productivity, and improve quality of life. From self-driving cars to virtual assistants, AI is becoming increasingly integrated into daily life, offering new possibilities and challenges for society.

AI encompasses a wide range of technologies, including machine learning, natural language processing, and computer vision. These technologies enable machines to learn from data, understand human language, and perceive their environment. AI has been applied to various fields, such as healthcare, finance, and manufacturing, leading to significant advancements and efficiencies. For example, AI-powered diagnostic tools can analyze medical images to detect diseases with greater accuracy, while predictive algorithms can help financial institutions identify fraudulent transactions.

However, the rise of AI also raises important ethical and societal considerations. Concerns about job displacement, privacy, and bias in AI algorithms have sparked debates about the responsible development and deployment of AI technologies. The potential for AI to perpetuate existing inequalities and create new forms of discrimination highlights the need for transparent and accountable AI systems. Policymakers, technologists, and ethicists must work together to address these challenges and ensure that AI benefits all members of society.

The future of AI holds both promise and uncertainty. As AI continues to advance, it is likely to transform various aspects of human life, from how we work to how we interact with each other. The potential for AI to augment human capabilities and solve complex problems is immense, but it also requires careful consideration and stewardship. The rise of AI represents a pivotal moment in history, shaping the trajectory of innovation and the future of humanity.

7

Chapter 7: The Exploration of Space

The exploration of space has been one of humanity's most ambitious and awe-inspiring endeavors. Since the mid-20th century, space exploration has expanded our understanding of the universe and our place within it. From the launch of the first artificial satellite to the landing of humans on the moon, space exploration has pushed the boundaries of human knowledge and capability. This chapter explores the milestones of space exploration and the quest to unlock the mysteries of the cosmos.

The space age began with the launch of Sputnik 1 by the Soviet Union in 1957, marking the first human-made object to orbit the Earth. This achievement ignited the space race, a period of intense competition between the United States and the Soviet Union to achieve dominance in space exploration. The United States responded with the Apollo program, culminating in the historic moon landing of Apollo 11 in 1969. Astronauts Neil Armstrong and Buzz Aldrin became the first humans to set foot on the lunar surface, symbolizing the triumph of human ingenuity and determination.

Space exploration has since evolved from a competition between superpowers to a collaborative global effort. International partnerships, such as the International Space Station (ISS), have brought together scientists and engineers from around the world to conduct research in microgravity and advance our understanding of space. Robotic missions, such as the Mars rovers and space telescopes like Hubble, have provided invaluable data about distant planets, stars, and galaxies. These missions have expanded our knowledge of the universe and inspired new generations of scientists and explorers.

The quest to explore space continues to drive innovation and technological advancements. The development of reusable rockets by private companies, such as SpaceX, has reduced the cost of space travel and opened new possibilities for commercial space exploration. Plans for crewed missions to Mars and the establishment of lunar bases are on the horizon, promising to further expand humanity's presence in space. The exploration of space represents a bold and exciting frontier, with the potential to unlock new discoveries and transform our understanding of the cosmos.

8

Chapter 8: The Evolution of Communication

The evolution of communication has been a defining aspect of human history, shaping the way we connect and share information. From the invention of writing to the rise of the internet, communication technologies have continually transformed societies and influenced cultural, political, and economic developments. This chapter explores the milestones in the evolution of communication and their impact on human civilization.

The invention of writing around 3500 BCE marked a significant turning point in human history. Writing enabled the recording and preservation of information, allowing knowledge to be transmitted across generations and distances. Early writing systems, such as cuneiform and hieroglyphics, were used for administrative, religious, and literary purposes. The development of alphabets and the spread of literacy further facilitated the exchange of ideas and the growth of civilizations.

The invention of the printing press by Johannes Gutenberg in the 15th century revolutionized communication and the dissemination of knowledge. The printing press made it possible to produce books and other written materials on a large scale, making information more accessible to a wider audience. The spread of printed materials played a crucial role in the Renaissance, the Reformation, and the Scientific Revolution, as ideas and discoveries could be shared and debated more widely. The printing press laid the groundwork for the modern information age.

The 20th century saw the rise of electronic communication technologies, such as the telephone, radio, and television. These innovations transformed the way people connected and consumed information, enabling real-time communication across vast distances. The advent of the internet in the late 20th century marked another transformative milestone, connecting people around the world and facilitating the exchange of information on an unprecedented scale. The internet has revolutionized industries, reshaped economies, and transformed daily life, making communication faster, easier, and more interactive.

The evolution of communication continues to advance with the development of new technologies, such as social media, mobile devices, and virtual reality. These innovations are changing the way we interact, share information, and experience the world. As communication technologies continue to evolve, they will undoubtedly shape the future of human civilization, influencing how we connect, collaborate, and understand each other.

9

Chapter 9: The Future of Education

The future of education is a topic of great importance and interest, as it holds the potential to shape the next generation and influence the direction of society. Education has always been a cornerstone of human development, fostering knowledge, skills, and critical thinking. As the world changes, so too must educational systems and practices evolve to meet the needs of a rapidly transforming society. This chapter explores the trends and innovations shaping the future of education and their implications for learners and educators.

The digital age has brought about significant changes in education, with technology playing an increasingly central role in the learning process. Online learning platforms, digital textbooks, and interactive educational tools have expanded access to education and provided new opportunities for personalized and self-directed learning. The rise of massive open online courses (MOOCs) has made high-quality education accessible to a global audience, breaking down geographical and economic barriers. These innovations have the potential to democratize education and empower learners to take control of their own learning journeys.

The future of education also involves rethinking traditional models of teaching and learning. The emphasis on standardized testing and rote memorization is giving way to more holistic and experiential approaches. Project-based learning, collaborative activities, and real-world problem-solving are becoming increasingly important, as they foster critical thinking, creativity, and practical skills. Educators are focusing on developing the whole person, nurturing not only academic knowledge but also social, emotional, and ethical competencies.

In addition to technological advancements, the future of education is being shaped by a growing recognition of the importance of lifelong learning. As the pace of change accelerates, individuals must continually update their skills and knowledge to stay relevant in the workforce and adapt to new challenges. Educational institutions and employers are recognizing the need for flexible and accessible learning opportunities that support continuous professional development and personal growth. Lifelong learning is becoming an essential component of a thriving and resilient society.

The future of education also involves addressing issues of equity and inclusion. Ensuring that all learners, regardless of their background, have access to high-quality education is a critical goal. Efforts to close achievement gaps, support diverse learning needs, and create inclusive learning environments are central to this mission. The future of education holds the promise of a more just and equitable society, where every individual has the opportunity to reach their full potential and contribute to the greater good.

10

Chapter 10: The Ethical Dimensions of Innovation

Innovation has always been a driving force behind human progress, pushing the boundaries of what is possible and improving the quality of life. However, with great power comes great responsibility. The ethical dimensions of innovation are critical considerations that must be addressed to ensure that technological advancements benefit society as a whole. This chapter explores the ethical challenges and considerations associated with innovation and the importance of responsible and inclusive practices.

One of the key ethical challenges of innovation is ensuring that new technologies are developed and deployed in ways that promote fairness and equity. Technological advancements can create significant benefits, but they can also exacerbate existing inequalities and create new forms of discrimination. Issues such as algorithmic bias, digital divide, and unequal access to technology must be addressed to ensure that innovation benefits all members of society. Inclusive design principles and practices that prioritize diversity and equity are essential to creating technologies that serve the needs of all people.

Privacy and data security are also critical ethical considerations in the age of digital innovation. The collection, storage, and use of personal data raise important questions about consent, transparency, and accountability.

Ensuring that individuals' privacy rights are respected and that data is handled responsibly is essential to building trust and protecting individual autonomy. Regulations and policies that safeguard privacy and promote data security are crucial components of ethical innovation.

Environmental sustainability is another important ethical dimension of innovation. The development and deployment of new technologies must consider their environmental impact and strive to minimize negative effects on the planet. Sustainable innovation practices that prioritize resource efficiency, renewable energy, and waste reduction are essential to addressing the environmental challenges of the 21st century. Balancing technological progress with ecological preservation is a key ethical responsibility.

Finally, the ethical dimensions of innovation involve fostering a culture of responsibility and accountability. Innovators, researchers, and organizations must be committed to ethical principles and practices, prioritizing the well-being of individuals and society. This includes engaging with stakeholders, considering the long-term implications of new technologies, and being transparent about risks and benefits. By fostering a culture of ethical innovation, society can ensure that technological advancements are guided by values that promote human dignity, justice, and the common good.

11

Chapter 11: The Role of Creativity and Art

Creativity and art have always been integral to the human experience, serving as powerful means of expression, communication, and connection. Throughout history, artists and creatives have challenged norms, inspired change, and provided insights into the human condition. This chapter explores the role of creativity and art in shaping societies and driving innovation, highlighting the enduring importance of the arts in an increasingly technological world.

Art has the unique ability to transcend boundaries and bring people together. It can evoke emotions, provoke thought, and inspire action. From the cave paintings of prehistoric times to contemporary digital art, creative expression has been a fundamental aspect of human culture. Artists have used their work to reflect on social issues, celebrate cultural heritage, and envision new possibilities. The power of art lies in its capacity to communicate complex ideas and foster empathy, making it a vital force for social change and progress.

Creativity and innovation are deeply interconnected. The arts encourage experimentation, exploration, and the questioning of established norms, which are essential elements of the innovation process. Many groundbreaking ideas and technologies have emerged from the intersection of art and science. For example, the Renaissance period saw a flourishing of creativity and intellectual curiosity, leading to significant advancements in various fields. Today, the integration of art and technology continues to drive innovation, as seen in fields such as digital media, design, and virtual reality.

The role of creativity and art in education and personal development cannot be overstated. Engaging in creative activities fosters critical thinking, problem-solving, and emotional intelligence. Arts education provides students with valuable skills and perspectives that are applicable across disciplines and in everyday life. In an era of rapid technological change, nurturing creativity is more important than ever, as it enables individuals to adapt, innovate, and thrive in a complex and dynamic world.

The future of creativity and art holds exciting possibilities. Advances in technology are opening new avenues for artistic expression and collaboration, from virtual art galleries to interactive installations. As society continues to evolve, the arts will remain a vital source of inspiration, innovation, and connection. Embracing the creative spirit and recognizing the importance of the arts are essential to building a vibrant and resilient future.

12

Chapter 12: The Philosophical Pursuit of Knowledge

The pursuit of knowledge is a fundamental aspect of human existence, driven by a deep curiosity and a desire to understand the world and our place within it. Philosophy, as the study of fundamental questions about existence, knowledge, and values, has played a central role in this pursuit. This chapter explores the evolution of philosophical thought and its impact on the development of human knowledge and society.

Ancient philosophers, such as Socrates, Plato, and Aristotle, laid the foundations for Western philosophy, exploring questions about ethics, metaphysics, and epistemology. Their inquiries into the nature of reality, the principles of reasoning, and the basis of moral conduct have had a profound influence on subsequent intellectual traditions. The works of these early philosophers continue to be studied and debated, providing valuable insights into the human condition and the quest for understanding.

Throughout history, philosophy has evolved in response to changing cultural, scientific, and intellectual contexts. The Enlightenment period, for example, saw the emergence of new philosophical ideas that emphasized reason, empiricism, and individual rights. Philosophers such as Descartes, Locke, and Kant challenged established doctrines and contributed to the development of modern science and political thought. The dialogue between philosophy and other disciplines, such as science, art, and literature, has enriched our understanding of the world and expanded the boundaries of knowledge.

In the contemporary era, philosophy continues to grapple with complex and pressing issues. The rapid advancement of technology, for example, raises important ethical and existential questions about the nature of humanity, the implications of artificial intelligence, and the impact of digital innovation on society. Philosophers engage with these questions, offering critical perspectives and frameworks for understanding the challenges and opportunities of the modern world. The interdisciplinary nature of contemporary philosophy fosters collaboration and dialogue across fields, enriching the pursuit of knowledge and addressing the multifaceted issues of our time.

The philosophical pursuit of knowledge is an ongoing journey, driven by the fundamental questions that have captivated human minds for millennia. As society continues to evolve, philosophy will remain a vital source of inquiry, reflection, and wisdom. By engaging with philosophical thought, individuals can gain deeper insights into themselves, their relationships, and the world around them, contributing to a richer and more meaningful existence.

13

Chapter 13: The Interplay of Science and Society

Science and society are intricately connected, with scientific advancements shaping societal developments and societal needs driving scientific inquiry. The interplay between science and society has been a driving force behind progress and innovation, influencing various aspects of human life, from health and technology to culture and ethics. This chapter explores the dynamic relationship between science and society and its impact on shaping the future.

Scientific discoveries have had profound effects on human health and well-being. Advances in medical science, for example, have led to the development of vaccines, antibiotics, and life-saving treatments, significantly improving life expectancy and quality of life. Public health initiatives, based on scientific research, have addressed major health challenges and promoted better health outcomes. The ongoing exploration of the human genome and the potential of personalized medicine hold promise for further advancements in healthcare, offering targeted and effective treatments for various conditions.

The relationship between science and technology is another key aspect of the interplay between science and society. Technological innovations, driven by scientific research, have transformed industries, economies, and daily life. The development of the internet, for instance, has revolutionized communication, commerce, and education, connecting people and information across the globe. Emerging technologies, such as artificial intelligence, renewable energy, and biotechnology, continue to shape the future, offering new opportunities and challenges for society.

Science also plays a critical role in addressing global challenges, such as climate change, resource depletion, and environmental sustainability. Scientific research provides the knowledge and tools needed to understand and mitigate the impact of human activities on the planet. Collaborative efforts between scientists, policymakers, and communities are essential to developing and implementing sustainable solutions that promote the well-being of both people and the environment. The integration of scientific knowledge into policy and decision-making processes is crucial for addressing complex and interconnected issues.

The interplay between science and society also involves ethical considerations and public engagement. Scientific advancements raise important ethical questions about the implications and applications of new technologies. Issues such as genetic engineering, data privacy, and artificial intelligence require careful consideration and inclusive dialogue to ensure that scientific progress aligns with societal values and priorities. Engaging the public in scientific discourse and fostering scientific literacy are essential for building trust and promoting informed decision-making.

14

Chapter 14: The Impact of Globalization

Globalization is a defining characteristic of the modern world, characterized by the increasing interconnectedness and interdependence of countries, economies, and cultures. The impact of globalization is far-reaching, influencing various aspects of human life, from trade and technology to culture and communication. This chapter explores the drivers and consequences of globalization and its implications for the future.

Economic globalization has been driven by the expansion of international trade, investment, and financial markets. Advances in transportation and communication technologies have facilitated the movement of goods, services, and capital across borders, creating a global economy. Multinational corporations and global supply chains have become integral to economic activity, connecting producers and consumers around the world. While economic globalization has contributed to economic growth and development, it has also raised concerns about inequality, labor rights, and environmental sustainability.

Cultural globalization involves the exchange and dissemination of cultural products, ideas, and practices across the world. The rise of the internet and digital media has accelerated the spread of cultural content, from music and films to fashion and cuisine. This cultural exchange has enriched societies, fostering diversity and cross-cultural understanding. However, it has also led to concerns about cultural homogenization and the erosion of local traditions and identities. Balancing the benefits of cultural exchange with the preservation of cultural heritage is an ongoing challenge.

Globalization has also influenced political and social dynamics. The interconnectedness of countries has led to greater collaboration and cooperation on global issues, such as climate change, public health, and security. International organizations, treaties, and agreements play a crucial role in addressing these challenges and promoting global governance. At the same time, globalization has also sparked debates about sovereignty, nationalism, and the impact of global forces on local communities. Navigating the complexities of globalization requires thoughtful and inclusive approaches that consider diverse perspectives and interests.

The impact of globalization on technology and innovation is significant. The global exchange of knowledge and expertise has accelerated technological advancements and fostered innovation ecosystems. Collaborative research and development efforts have led to breakthroughs in various fields, from medicine to renewable energy. However, the digital divide and unequal access to technology remain pressing issues, highlighting the need for policies and initiatives that promote digital inclusion and ensure that the benefits of globalization are shared equitably.

15

Chapter 15: The Future of Humanity

The future of humanity is a topic of profound importance and speculation, encompassing the potential paths and possibilities for human development and progress. As we navigate an era of rapid change and unprecedented challenges, envisioning the future involves reflecting on our values, aspirations, and responsibilities. This chapter explores the potential future scenarios for humanity and the key factors that will shape our collective destiny.

Technological advancements will undoubtedly play a central role in shaping the future of humanity. Innovations in fields such as artificial intelligence, biotechnology, and renewable energy hold the promise of addressing some of the most pressing challenges we face, from climate change to healthcare. The potential for human enhancement through technologies like gene editing and neural interfaces raises important ethical and philosophical questions about what it means to be human. As we explore these possibilities, it is essential to consider the potential impacts on society and ensure that technological advancements are used to promote human flourishing and well-being.

Environmental sustainability will also be a critical factor in shaping the future of humanity. Addressing climate change, preserving biodiversity, and managing natural resources responsibly are essential to ensuring a healthy and resilient planet for future generations. The transition to a sustainable future will require concerted efforts from governments, businesses, and individuals, as well as innovative solutions that balance economic growth with environmental stewardship. The quest for sustainability will be a defining challenge of the 21st century, shaping the trajectory of human development.

Social and political dynamics will continue to evolve, influencing the future of humanity. Issues such as inequality, migration, and governance will require thoughtful and inclusive approaches that prioritize the well-being of all people. The promotion of human rights, social justice, and democratic values will be essential to building a more equitable and just world. International cooperation and collaboration will be crucial in addressing global challenges and fostering a sense of shared responsibility and common purpose.

Ultimately, the future of humanity will be shaped by our collective choices and actions. As we navigate an era of rapid change and uncertainty, it is important to reflect on our values, aspirations, and responsibilities. By embracing innovation, fostering creativity, and prioritizing ethical considerations, we can work towards a future that promotes human dignity, well-being, and the common good. The journey ahead is full of possibilities, and the echoes of the past will continue to guide and inspire us as we shape the future.

Echoes of the Future: A Philosophical Journey Through History and Innovation

In "Echoes of the Future," embark on a captivating exploration of humanity's enduring quest for knowledge, progress, and meaning. This thought-provoking book takes you on a journey through the pivotal moments and ideas that have shaped our world, from the dawn of civilization to the cutting-edge innovations of today.

Each chapter delves into a distinct era, uncovering the transformative events, thinkers, and inventions that have defined human history. From the birth of writing and the rise of ancient empires to the intellectual fervor of the Enlightenment and the technological marvels of the Digital Age, "Echoes of the Future" weaves together the threads of history and philosophy to reveal the profound interconnectedness of past, present, and future.

Throughout the book, you will encounter the visionaries and pioneers who dared to challenge the status quo and push the boundaries of what is possible.

Their stories inspire us to reflect on our own journey and consider the ethical, social, and environmental implications of our actions. As we navigate an era of rapid change and uncertainty, "Echoes of the Future" invites us to embrace the spirit of curiosity, creativity, and innovation that has driven humanity forward.

Richly detailed and elegantly written, "Echoes of the Future" is a celebration of human achievement and a call to action for a more thoughtful and sustainable future. Whether you are a history enthusiast, a philosophy aficionado, or simply curious about the world around you, this book offers a profound and engaging exploration of the forces that have shaped our past and continue to shape our future.

www.ingramcontent.com/pod-product-compliance
Lightning Source LLC
LaVergne TN
LVHW020501080526
838202LV00057B/6095